TECHNO POETRY

Also by Peggy C. Hall

Gus 'n Us
with Frank Wendeln

In Case of Bears

Techno Poetry
Seasonal Amnesia

&

Not Always What it Seems

by

Peggy C. Hall

A RILEY HALL PUBLICATION

2010

A RILEY HALL PUBLICATION

Visit our website at www.rileyhall.com

Library of Congress Cataloging-in-Publication Data is available.
ISBN#978-0-9665310-9-1

First Published June 2010

Drawing by Beverly Frost used by kind permission
Book Layout & Cover Photography/Design by Frank Wendeln

To Sandy, the leader of the band, and, best of all,

My Very Own Majorette

*I watch her lift higher, high
her stick batons, from earth to sky,
simple branches, dew still clinging,
sequined in the early light.*

*Then she spins them, left to right,
winding up the spiders' threads:
gauzy cloaks between the trees,
costumes made in haste last night.*

*On she whirls them, spinning faster
than the cotton-candy maker,
till she throws them, wonder worker,
giving me a real good show,*

*and safety, too. That's why she wields
rod and staff and wand before us,
leads me through, furling webs,
twirling the world in front of me.*

TABLE OF CONTENTS

Techno Poetry: Seasonal Amnesia

Techno Poetry (Unplugged): Not Always What it Seems

The Poet's Preface

In 2007, the initial proposal for *Techno Poetry* came from Travis Neff, whom I call "The Light Man." Travis is one of the founders as well as the Executive Director of the Crystal Parrot Players (CPP). He is a vital part of Miami's eclectic, innovative, young living arts community, working to create unique theater experiences. His question to me: "What if hand-picked dancers, singers, actors, performance artists took 25 of your poems and, self-directed, interpreted them for the stage in any form they chose? With lots of stunning effects, of course!"

My "Yes, yes" led to one of the most liberating times of my life. Letting my words go. My sole directive was that the words of each poem be presented in at least one form: printed in the program, voiced-over, acted live, projected on a screen, or sung. I deliberately chose not to attend rehearsals, gave no comments on any of the poems (except when bribed with food), saw and heard nothing until opening night, when, under the finely wired stage managers, sisters Monica and Veronica …

Laverne preached the gospel of groceries. Ana became a wild Hungarian dancer whirling in an inverted hoop skirt and top hat. Jason wrote and directed a playlet for the ensemble, based on the theme "Seasonal Amnesia" and other poems about Miami's bi-polarism. Ray and Sole choreographed and soulfully danced to Satie's doleful music and two voiced-over poems.

T.L. took a road trip to Idaho, then became a reluctant gardener, an angry Miami weeder. Ellen metamorphosed from composer of a hymn she sang *acappella* to a belated Elvis worshipper to a psychiatrist counseling Gus, our green teddy bear, spilling his guts. Belly dancing in multi-colored veils the hues of parrots was Hanan's speciality. Rudi played both the thug and the rape victim in Spoken Word mode. Teresa and Rudi went for broke, hip-dancing off the stage. All with lots of techno effects by Travis, of course! "Intelligent" lights, strobes and sparklers, voices off, screen projections, prayers with candles and smudge sticks, *jembe* rhythms, mini-dramas offstage and on, Monopoly money and roses flung into the audience.

In 2008, CPP was eager to produce a second *Techno Poetry*. But, out of funds for a large cast, let alone expensive "effects," Travis announced, "We'll unplug *Techno Poetry!*" So *Techno Poetry: Not Always What It Seems* became our theme, our title, our new m.o. Under simple lighting, just five actors filled New Theatre's bare proscenium stage with their superb selves in monologues, duets, ensemble chants. Laverne channeled pistol-packin' Calamity Jane, then later expired as a 95-year-old after reliving "dreamy" moments. Odell channeled the "mad, bad" Lord Byron, then became an Eastern Kentucky hill man rescuing a stray kitten on his way to the hospital. An oculist, "Doctor" Rudi diagnosed psychedelic eye problems in his office. Later, as a slacker, Rudi whined about August's hot "cat days." Jennifer talked "nice" about her ex-husband before she went back in time to reveal the secrets behind Fanny Brawne's brief love affair with her fiancée John Keats. Laverne and Odell literally "jazzed" up the physics-philosophy-heavy poem "Rock of Ages." When the whole ensemble went canoeing in the Everglades on the ever-changing River of Grass, we Miamians were once again reminded that life is "Not Always What It Seems."

My purpose in publishing these poems is to continue encouraging creativity in their interpretation and performance. As a young teacher beginning in the 60s, I remember how much fun it was for my high school kids to create choral readings of old English ballads (who wants to play the ghost?), Langston Hughes' lyrics, Carl Sandburg's "Jazz Fantasia." In the 80s and 90s, my contributions as musical coordinator and pianist in Sandra Riley's productions of *The Fantasticks, The Madwoman of Chaillot, On the Verge,* and *Search for Signs of Intelligent Life in the Universe* amped up my love of theater. Hey, watching Travis light up my poems in *Techno Poetry* and *Techno Poetry (Unplugged)* was much more fun than any old poetry reading at a book store.

Peggy C. Hall
Miami, Florida
May 2010

Production Histories

TECHNO POETRY: SEASONAL AMNESIA

Techno Poetry: Seasonal Amnesia, by Peggy C. Hall was produced by the Crystal Parrot Players with Miami Contemporary Dance Company in association with Miami Light Project with the support of Miami-Dade Country Department of Cultural Affairs. It was presented at the Miami Contemporary Dance Company's Intimate Movement Lab in Miami Beach, Florida, (Ray Sullivan, Artistic Director and Lead Choreographer) on June 22 & 23, 2007. Artistic Director was Sandra Riley; Technical Director was Travis Neff; Lighting Design was by Kevin Roman; Set Design was by Tate Tenorio; Sound Design by Natan Samuels; Recording by Nate Rausch and Video by Felix Becerra. Stage Managers were Monica Soderman and Veronica Sierra-Soderman.

The ensemble of actors, dancers, voice-over artists included: Teresa Barceló, T.L. Brown, Robert E. Dorfman, Rudi Goblen, Gus Greenbear, Peggy C. Hall, Ellen Haynes, Laverne Lewis-Cuzzocrea, Tiffany Hanan Madera, Ana Mendez, Jennifer Stewart, Jason Stoetzer, Ray Sullivan and Soledad Centurión Vedro.

TECHNO POETRY (UNPLUGGED): NOT ALWAYS WHAT IT SEEMS

Techno Poetry (Unplugged): Not Always What It Seems, by Peggy C. Hall was produced by the Crystal Parrot Players and presented at New Theatre in Coral Gables, Florida (Ricky J. Martinez, Artistic Director and Eileen Suarez, Managing Director) on July 12, 2008. The Director was Sandra Riley and the Technical Director was Travis Neff.

The cast was as follows:
Rudi Goblen
Gus Greenbear
Laverne Lewis-Cuzzocrea
Odell Rivas
Jennifer Stewart

Seasonal Amnesia

Beverly Frost

A Medicine Wheel Prayer

I stand before the stones in prayer,
in easy morning or hard-stormed night.
Enclosing, curling smoke around me
readies my prayer, steadies me groundward,
wisps me skyhooked, lifts me up,
sage-sense quickened, to learn the birds.

Help me see their unheard songs
that beat their way over water,
my path today through mind and matter,
sense and soul.

School me towards a loving heart.

The Miami Circle*

I am dreaming of circles, rings
of neon hoops around our Moon,
whose pock-marked, cicatrized face
illuminates this medicine wheel,
shaken from its old, old bed.
Two thousand years the site has lain
sleeping sacred under quiet earth.

Now I'm seeing ancient tribal scars
scooped and shaped around the rim:
aureoles on this Great Mother,
opened to life by praying men
helping Solar Father join his bride
through her limestone-hymened skin,
pressing inward, fulfilling life,
wedding
fire-ringed Earth
to rainbowed Sky.

*A prehistoric Tequesta Indian archaeological site on the banks of the
Miami River, Miami, Florida.

A Tribute to Charlotte d'Amboise, in Broadway's "Contact"

I dream of you leaping, levitating,
a dandelion blowball, in parachute dress
of chiffon that falls slowly, bones waiting
for the long gown to drift down, to caress
your hips, thighs, long legs, to acquiesce
to gravity. Thank God I saw you dance.
I begin to fathom the old romance

of human and divine, of space and time
moving united in toes, muscles, arms.
A dance is an ancient pantomime
of creation, of change from calm to alarm,
a metamorphosis, like a bee swarm
that quietly works and hums in its hive
until it is moved to act, instinctive,

as dervishes do, hands pointed toward earth
and heaven, chant-singers whirling into trance.
Belly dancers sign the zone of birth
from horizontal sways to small, nuanced
tremors that sweep, sinuous, like a *fer-de-lance*
across the ground. But why the veil, the hood,
the mask? Dancer as demon, goddess, the Good?

➤

Like mating rites of the birds and the beasts
dances labeled Round and Square, called jigs and reels
or flings and romps (these sound like imps unleashed!)
all, all transform, energize. All reveal
a primal Force, in our free but fixed quadrille.
I never saw my mother dance. However,
I'll bet she hoofed the Charleston. With fervor.

And you, Charlotte d'Amboise, what do you say?
Are you too busy to philosophize?
What role are you playing now on Broadway?
What tired cast was struck by your sweet surprise?
What new playgoers will you mesmerize?
You told the *Times*: "I'm the replacement queen."
Tonight, if I'm lucky, you'll dance in my dreams.

Published in Penumbra *2003*

Ah, Sweet Mystery of Life

I had a ruffled sundress, I was five or six or so,
I posed, looked up at brother, pointed all my toes,
bothered busy Daddy taking snapshots white and black,
whined, "Why doesn't the picture ever show my back?"
Finally, Mother turned me round, in tired self-defense—

I've disliked all photo shoots ever, ever since.

Published in Möbius *2003 and online* Möbius *2004*

Bridges

Once we counted bridges, looked right and left.
For each one crossed, we earned two extra points.
The game—our mother's ploy—served as constraint
against sororicide, though Brother, deft
with secret punches, numbed my arm. That gift
Mom had of spanning sibling rifts—bridge joints
not made of steel but strings of words the faint-
mouthed would not say, could not craft—
that voice is gone.
                    So now we only drive
on roads that parallel the banks. No links,
connections, bonds, or ties, just concrete lanes
that take us north and south through daily lives
that shun the risks that gamblers take. We sink
no pylons, shun each ford. The gulf remains.

Published in PA Prize Poems *2004*
and in Poets at Work *2006*

A Chant Royal for the King

I watched an Elvis special on t.v.
and found, much to my surprise, my chagrin,
I loved that young, hillbilly boy. To me,
pushing sixty-four, sporting double chins,
he looked so young, fresh—gasp—innocent
(if innocence is not just a figment
of the mind, but really lives in the soul).
I recalled the outcry, that rigmarole
of nicknaming him "Elvis the Pelvis."
You can run this up the old flagpole:
It's never too late to love Elvis.

He is now simply called "the King," but I see
him not as King Arthur, but more as Merlin,
a shape-shifter. Wouldn't you agree
they both could appear in another's skin?
Man turned to bird, white turned to black? Ancient
mysteries, magical "soul" music, potent
Gospels of Druids or slaves, cajoling
the people to praise Nature, consoling
the lovelorn with a song from old Memphis?
Yes, both "charming" men I now extol:
It's never too late to love Elvis.

➤

What if we, like Merlin, could live life free
of time, could grow younger, not older, spin
through the 90s, the 80s, then be
there at Graceland that August day when
Death stepped on the King's "Blue Suede Shoes"? In moments
like those, I wish I could say I'd cried, or I went
into mourning with the world of rock-and-roll.
Mid-career teacher, occupied with control,
supporting my son in the metropolis
of Miami. . . thirty-five, I didn't show
it's never too late to love Elvis.

At 18, I was no groupie
of the King's, since I couldn't imagine
dancing to t.v.-censored Elvis Presley,
but when I saw Richard, hunkerin' at the drive-in
"Big Top" (my ex looked just like E.P.), intent
on chrome that mirrored bedroom eyes, ardent
pouty lips, long sideburns, duck-tail hair (coal
black at 25) . . . . New town, "wicked" beau—
I embraced them both. Eloped. Became less
strait-laced and realized, though I was slow,
it's never too late to love Elvis.

Mississippi, Tennessee, Kentucky:
All southern states, lots of hills, lots of kin,
where Elvis and I were born, but bred to flee
poor-folks' small towns. The world called us "bumpkins."
Maybe that's why I was no celebrant
of mountain ways, worked to lose my accent,
short-changed my son for a fatter payroll.
When I see old movies like *King Creole*
I admit my failings; I was remiss.
So though I'm no angel with wings, aureole,
it's never too late to love Elvis.

What is my mission now, just one bright goal
(besides seeing his birthplace, up north at Tupelo)?
To play all his songs, both obscure and timeless,
say "Love Me Tender" and "Stay Away, Joe."
It's never too late to love Elvis.

Published in Sincerely Elvis: An Anthology of Original Poems about Elvis Aaron Presley. *Hot Biscuit Productions 2005*

Room Enough and Time

Yellow-belly tiger cat on the sky-
light laps dew, paws splayed
in age like me, sprawled
in my green-sling chair, red-ruled
pad primed

puttering down
the cat-contented words
that look through stained-
glass panes to Florida, then back again
to picture books and prints of cougar
horse and fish

or praying over
piano keys, new plastic teeth
in mahogany gums and pedals long
tarnished by my very toes.

And where are you?

In your studio,
close enough for minds
not to mind
the spaces we keep.

Published in Poetry of the People 2002; WITA Triumphs 2003;
Poets at Work 2005

Meta4play

Foreplay: warm up on scales, athlete's stretches, contractor's
    forms for sidewalks not laid, boat's still in dry-dock
    to lower away, heat up the oven 350 degrees

Coupling: aria in the ears, fluids from the runner,
    concrete poured on each crack and crevice, deep dives
    the rudder high flies the sail, buns that rise and
    rise and rise

Afterglow: applause still echoes on vacated stage, muscles
    released hamstrings sore, walkway smooth and bright
    renewed, harbored sheets that dry on the
    mast, sweets that surfeit all appetites of art

La Souvenir avec Satie

Your silly simple scar from boyhood games
says, wrist white, "You will see me in your dreams,"
draws me always past tanned or winter face
to find that underfleshed fault, retrace

Satie shadows piano played, as if to seep
between the cracks between the keys, Delphic deep,
notes released to hang in your chained smoke
then fall into our dusky wine, an unspoken

moment between the lust and leaving.
Wet canvas on the easel, my eyes drying
in green. Your overcoat, brown, waits in the hall
with art's-sake sleeves to hide the blemish I recall.

Published in Common Threads *2003;* Poets at Work *2005*

Go, Artful Envoy

Go, painting from the past.
With sagging canvas, faded oils,
tell him you have returned at last,
the final piece. If he recoils,
be brave, be undeterred,
remind him of his parting words:

"Never give my art away."
He said that on the day
he hung you, colors deep
shadowed so to make me weep
from loving him, his lovely gift
that he left me when he left.

Join the letters I returned
long ago, through the mail,
and the portraits that I learned
to hate, images of me unveiled
except my eyes, clothed in love,
garments I could not remove.

But if he asks, "What took so long?"
be strangely silent. That's not wrong,
my weathered friend. You so did grace
my screened porch, that rained-on space,
until today. So go now,
to show I kept my word—somehow.

Published in the Acorn: A Journal of the Western Sierra *2003*

15

All Our Ages
(to my son turning forty)

Seven pictures show your first haircut:
From teary-eyed baby to suckered youth
you toddled out the door, laughing lollipopped mouth.

This winter your grandfather quietly died
the day after we looked at snapshots of his life.
Teary-eyed, he smiled at 90 years of folly.

And I? There is 70, not far in my future.
Most pictures reveal my soft spots of age.
Teary-eyed?

Only at the movies.

Idaho Second-homecoming

There is the trip west—
and there is the ranch,
and both are good, but different,

              the same.

On Interstate 90, or 80, or 10
corn high, corn low, being danced, being hoed
we've seen the fields, a decade of roads.

But past and beyond the Badlands
or mesas
looproads to monuments,
towers, and sites,
cow-town saloons, Wall Drug overnight,
Death Valley so hot good God in late June . . .

There is the ranch
twelve miles up from town
ten degrees cooler, or more in the shade.
We finally see deer, on Big Cedar Road
white flowers high meadowed,
though the chicory's late.
Nez Perce Appaloosas
far down by the river.

It's greener this year
still raining like Spring
at our ranch with two horses
three cats and three dogs
who rush out to bark
then remember us
well.

Published in In Case of Bears *2006*

Have a Bloomin' Happy Birthday!

My garden is growing a party for me,
baring blooms under Miami sun:
Angel Trumpets with brassy throats Swingtime
Big Band for bougainvillaea, draped like peplumed
Flamenco skirts, red over purple over gold.

Exotic crotons sway and breezily dance,
a waltz by the Dreadlocks, reggae for the Queen
("Victoria's Hat," she's called). Not by chance,
Patti Ponytail palm (strands droplet-festooned),
flaunts her punky cowlick in unfettered joy.

And plants struggling, stripped by Fall's hurricanes?
"Crossandra," I say, "You're coming back! From sprigs!
And you, Yesterday-Today-and-Tomorrow,
have three green sprouts on your bony twigs,
harbinger buds for Spring's birthday season."

What Flower Power?

Weeds are at the root of all my weevils.

A weed is a poised blade,
ready to run through the roses:
To the victor belong the soils!

One entry for weed in a dictionary
(Etymological):
"Root unknown."

The best of all passable worlds
for the gardener who
can't see beyond the end of her rows
(oops! She sowed wild oats,
and didn't beware of mulch bearing "gifts")
is a place where
she can pull weeds up by their shoot caps,
be weedless and fancy free,
with no ants in her plants,
since hell hath no fury like a woman weed worn.

A weed by any other name
still smells
like feet.

Seasonal Amnesia

Miami summer skies, puff-bloated black
by three o'clock, chase faces red or pale
from pink *cabañas* by the pools, assail
slow picnic parties with swift thunder cracks
and scare us all with lightning rickrack
quick-basted down from sky to sea—I shall
desist from piling up these dire details
and simply ask, Knowing this, who'd come back?

The old, who rise to take diurnal walks,
the young, who bed the day until sunset,
some Witnesses, who knock from door to door,
flambéed tourists, who come to shop and gawk,
and optimistic natives, who "forget"
each daily storm and crowd the blonde seashore.

Urban Pastoral

"I thought of questions that have no reply."

Robert Frost

Hunkered down, with still hands cupped to smoke,
though it seemed to me he held a flute
or juice-harp I had child-seen many times
sideways hummed by mountain men Spring met
in country graveyards, corralling in our clan
of hill-born kin. But then I saw the wisp
snake up. A stranger crouched in our back yard.

His shirt looked white on white, for Florida sun
blurred it so. I'd left my glasses on my desk,
just walked outside to turn the clothes to "DRY,"
used to waving, tendrilled ferns, green palms,
or deep-blood cardinals bathing in the pond
that Harold stacked the slated rocks to make.
Used to sirens heard but blocked from view,
and school bells squiring all the children on,
and alley trucks that moved the margins clean.
We'd raised wood fences, latticed them still higher.
The bougainvillaea thorned them all around.

Except one gate. "His entry, Ma'am," they said,
arrested in their brisk, policing scan

by my babble, like a sheep's head, all jaw:
"No, I never saw him clearly, or even move,
approach our deck, gazebo door, or house.
I was surprised, you see, that he came at all.
I turned, as in a dream, to make this call,
and rushed to bolt the doors, the three of them,
afraid to look again, to see him where . . . .

But yes, I see your point. So peaceful here.
Sure, he could hoist himself up six feet high,
and just be glad to rest beside the pool.
Convenience stores don't let you loiter long.
Oh no! I never saw the way he left . . . ."

The laundry lay all day, forgotten, wet,
though Harold came, to build atop the gate,
while, hunkered down to think it through,
I smoldered—angry, scared, defiant, sad.
Who was the wolf-snake? The shepherd? The lamb?

Published in Frost Notes *2005*

Used Goods Choriambics

Locks unlocked then the door closing she sweeps gladly into her house
Ten o'clock and two hours waiting for year's end where alone she'll hear
Rockets burst with the horns honking so TV is my friend tonight
Parties suck so she thinks purse and her dress flying off arms and breasts
Sweats for comfort the bed calls but she swears Hell what has happened here
Eyes assaulted a tire rod on the mattress who has raped my house
Jolting rush to the rear porch where a hole gapes where the Hell's the door
Common crime the police drone as she steps hatefully back inside
Knowing how she will feel breathing the air left by the thug who's gone.

Miami Daily, at Dusk

I hear wild parrots' squawk parade.
No serenade,
no dulcet tones,
nor polyphones.
Just Punch 'n Judy wacked-out screams,
in steady streams
from lava throats
like knights' surcoats.
They bully me, their peasant slave
until I wave,
then hold my seared,
admonished ears.

Five Tropical Haiku

Omnipresent Eye-
Ball in a Florida sky
even when it rains.

Bougainvillaea
flower cascades preen like cats'
thorns sheathed in plush paws.

Poinciana blooms,
like royal progresses, leave
as October nods.

A parrot circus
entertains every evening
on our fruited trees.

Ballooning moon lifts
languidly from beach cradle
and turtle eggs shine.

#5 published in Grandmother Earth *2004*

My Feelings Bared

I need to fatten on thimbleberries and grubs
pass day's hours in blowy meadow crossings
scratch my back forever on trees
snuffle up the scent of winter's new cave

I want to fish in the pools
of notime, nolimit
or contemplate my claws
and cuff the cubs—as mother bears do.

Instead

I am baited by expectant, dutiful dogs
that yap and harry
just one more jig
O funny bruin
backed to the wall

Shall I grin and bear it?
Growl for one last smoke?

Or just bare my carnivores
and chew them all up
into gobbets?

Published in In Case of Bears *2006*

Sunday Morning Service at Publix

"And the peace of God, which passeth all understanding."
Philippians 4:7

I love the quiet aisles, Muzak hymning droneward
over shelf stockers yawning,
on their knees,
paying for late Saturday nights
in pre-dawn communion with Melba toast.

The deli rail is clear, uncrowded,
as I bow my head to praise the cheeses
that the net-hatted priestess slices oh so wafer-thin,
and I bless her and her Spanglish
I only half understand.

Then move on to the butcher,
elder bloodied carver
of the loins, breasts, and thighs
he will offer me in sacrifice
for my next week's suppers.

The bakery smells heavenly,
but I roll past it to Produce
where tomatoes need my prayers:
Lead me not into temptation.

Soon I'm with the checker,
who punches in my tithe,
as she dreads the later masses
who will strain her
"Nice day" benediction.

When the usher bags me out
with the groceries rightly wrapped
I know the peace that passeth all,

understanding that I must hurry
before the ice cream melts.
    Amen.

Sylvia's Prayer

To thank you, God, I lay bare
the truths that Spider taught,
when I was young, made fresh aware
what Mother Earth had wrought.

She birthed the eggs from silken sacs,
eight legs on each small frame,
for perfect balance front and back,
renewed if one went lame.

I watched you, Spider, on my knees,
you spun both low and high,
you sidled down from Heaven's trees,
connecting me to sky.

O Spider, wide-eyed, lacking lashes,
did you see me there,
as you survived, stored flies in caches,
inbound with silver hair?

Now, Great Spirit, stick my soul
anew to webbed Earth's wheel,
accept my praise as I extol
the patterns you reveal.

Published in Poets at Work *2005;* In Case of Bears *2006*

Grand Tour Villanelle

You must travel, all haphazard, never mind the weather chart.
Learn some cattycornered secrets, walk the world's circumference.
Cut through then to center, bringing back your journeyed heart.

Though Easter's here, rain and slosh, muddy ways, you should depart,
stuffed with eggs, curious lies, and adolescent impudence.
You must travel, all haphazard, never mind the weather chart.

Meander in summer on Mozart rivers, aired with counterpart,
grow too many leaves and loves of incautious indulgence.
Cut through then to center, bringing back your journeyed heart.

Only pause to gather melons, feast on yellow autumn's corn, and take part
with bonfired shadows, to celebrate fading incandescence.
You must travel, all haphazard, never mind the weather chart.

As Grail knights, on cold earth and breath, yet rode, brave and stalwart,
crawl if you must, warm in your mind, no little surrender to winter indolence.
Cut through then to center, bringing back your journeyed heart.

Elemental tour now finished? No, that's only true in art.
In life, there is love's trip, longing for quintessence.
You must travel, all haphazard, never mind the weather chart,
then circle round to center, bringing back your journeyed heart.

What's Left

I hope that I can find you
over the moon and back,
to watch the sunbow shine through
if life turns wrecken black.

But all I know, my loveling,
is that Now, this starry day,
must burn, with comets trailing,
all but love away.

Techno Poetry
(Unplugged)

NOT ALWAYS WHAT IT SEEMS

In the Moment

No more anticipation, no more wait

For the zoo lion's snarling, spitting wrath

For hurricane surges that inundate

For roller coasters laughing you to depths

For dying friends singing last Irish breaths

For the play to start, with you/me in the cast

For pain medications, for weddings of worth

Thank God, they're here—the words—at last.

LOVING AND LEAVING

Nuptials

"The imagination spans beyond despair,
Outpacing bargain, vocable, and prayer."

Hart Crane

Imagine, small as an eyelash, a bridge
inscribed upon a grain of rice to throw
atop a lily-of-the-valley show:
Mall-order bride 'n groom, with arched treillage
that mimics Gothic ceiling's challenge
to eyes that leap from pyloned stones to O
my God that vault of sky, acrylic bow
that prisms down through space to seaside moorage.

Their pontoon bridge awaits. So pay the toll
that blesses two to cross between the themes
(sonatas have those parts where links must fit)
and make the passage work toward coda's goal:
The slough of despond changed to joy, a dream
transformation, with Love as the transit.

Sky Blue Waters Award 2003
Writer's Digest *Award 2004*

Not Always What It Seems

The day that I was married

        (it wasn't in a church)

at an old, country courthouse

        (the room was small—a closet?)

the preacher said, "I'm Presley"

        (not Elvis—his name was Amos).

I was young and so excited

        (not of legal age),

scared by the file clerks

        (they let my forgery pass)

who lingered on my clothes

        (my coat and shoes were black).

They witnessed some brief words

        (they stood out in the hall),

quickly wished us on our way

        (Presley left to scrum up business).

The town was LaFollette

        (maybe it was Jellico)

across state lines and curvy mountains

        (the ride home made me sick).

My mother wasn't there

        ("a funeral" I lied to her).

My bride night lay ahead

        (a station wagon in the graveyard).

I went on to college
                    (I wasn't pregnant then).
The paper announced the marriage
                    (six months later, end of June).
I was happy being married
                    (it didn't last).

I Just Spoke Nicely to My Ex on the Telephone

To make a better grade, recall those old Xs.
Take it way back, to class rooms, lovers, and times
your simple self acted so reflexively.

We blame that on youth, which is not a crime
unless you shoplifted from nickel-and-dime
stores, while neglecting to learn those complex
equations the math teacher thought sublime.

"To make a better grade, recall all your Xs,"
she wrote, the red ink prescribing Rxs
to prevent the ills she foresaw, rhymeless
but real as a blow to your solar plexus.

So, take it way back, to rooms and failed lovers. Time
to reflect, my friend, on mistakes you signed
off on, like X kisses in mash notes you sent
to your best friend's beau.

Okay, that's slimy,
but your simple self acted so reflexively,
like eating the super-size at the triplex.

Hey, it's midlife! Aren't we all in our prime?
Go on, mark your ballot for crooks, reduced taxes.
We'll blame that on age, which is not a crime—
unless it is.

I propose this paradigm
(measured, like carpet, for the new annex):
Don't just go through life's motions, like pan-
tomime.

Study bridge, football, tic-tac-toe. Call an ex-
Yeah, make a better grade.

Behind a Museum Door in England

Lavenham: "the most complete medieval town"
where I learned *Twinkle, twinkle, little star*
was written by Jane Taylor, a local Miss,
whose nursery rhyme and spinsterhood gown
seemed piously right in her Dissenter's armoire.
But then, behind the museum door, was this
odd, *How-I-wonder-what-you-are* poem.
By a feminist Jane, or just a whim?
Entitled "The Disillusioned Bride,"
the poem has the young wife demystify
her young marriage. She speaks plainly, to guide.
No lines like *Up above the world so high,*
but earthy words of ill conduct, male pride . . .
This truth-poem is *Like a diamond in the sky.*

Ectoplasmic

Skylight, skyfright,
uncommon view I see tonight—
for there, against the convex dusk,

double-shadowed doves brusquely
clack their concave beaks
like ghosts refracting weird
obliques.

Henry, in Love, at Leeds Castle

"No mirth can make me fain,
Till that we meet again."
Henry VIII, "To His Lady" (Anne Boleyn)

It was her slender, freakish hands I loved,
that extra pinky I adored pushing
between my puckered lips, often pursed to move
into a reddened pout that matched the flush
then blooming on my face. I stroked Anne's lithesome neck
and laughed as she covered the mole, that flaw
of strawberry size, quite like the harsh peck
an enflamed rooster might make. "Devil's Paw"
some would hiss, twice marked on face and hand.
'though slander may lie in Future's bed, not here
at Leeds, with black swans on the lake, our blend
of sweated-spice, myself perfumed as Sonneteer . . . .
Love spells quite real, not made by witchery,
but by eye, nape, ear, mouth, hand mystery.

Calamity Jane's Lament

Folks said I wailed—for sure, that ain't true,
I was too busy, his blood on my arm—
My teeth were rippin' his shirt into strips
to tie up my Bill, his sweet face still warm.

One said I stole . . . Oh damn, how he lied!
Why would I pilfer Wild Bill's gold dust pouch,
when all that I wanted was my gold charm
that lay with the nuggets, worn from his touch?

His new wife said I "departed from truth."
She rode, so dainty, from Bill's Boot Hill grave.
But I knew he'd called me his "Bullwhackin' Bird,"
and loved his Canary, who couldn't behave.

But mostly who lied was murderin' McCall,
who left Hickok dyin' on the bar floor.
Jack said he saw me pick up Wild Bill's cards,
aces and eights, as he ran out the door.

Jack said I was drunk, or too yeller to shoot,

The truth is much tougher, damned hard to tell:

My anger at Bill for turnin' his back

blinded my aim—and put me in hell.

Martha Jane Canary Burke (1852-1903) was a famous frontier markswoman, whose name was often linked to James Butler "Wild Bill" Hickok. She and Bill are both buried in the cemetery at Deadwood, South Dakota.

Deadwood Writing Contest Award
Published online at cityofdeadwood.com
and In Case of Bears *by Peggy C. Hall 2006*

On the Opening of Lord Byron's Burial Vault 15 June 1938

Hypochondriac? Psychodramatist?
Good Greek words to try the tongues of clerics
who lay these polysyllables broadside
my Scottish soul. Bard or beast? Most say both,
unbless me e'en inside this family vault,
where vandals stript steel cherubims, stole the
very cover plate from the box that gaols my bones.
George Gordon, Lord Byron, Noel Byron:
I boast these names from mother, father, wife.
I'll wager you call me Juan, Manfred, Cain—
Let's drink to all who have listened thus far!
Seize on this Gothicism, if you will:
My birth-lamed foot lies severed 'low my corpse.
Who straightened its crypt-swimming through eternity?
(Parse my play *Deformed Transformed.* My heirs could
use a rise in gilt.) Shelley claimed I was
no Platonist, but 'llowed, in truth, how oft
I tried to launch Hellenic ships. Augusta
half understood my "shadows of beauty,"
though Hobhouse laughed. We raised another draught
to Greek Independence—till we spewed out,
in watery death, our memoired meals. Fire took
my last papers. Murray made sure of that,

➤

▶

muffled as he was in mediocrity.
I shun such masks, having hawked the truth
of loving much . . . my fond pet bear
and sundry more, for 'Love dwells not in our will,'
but in blind eyes, clapped ears and parts, in tongues
that lick the dregs of life's lost child . . . Break off!
and take your relics back that reek of must,
that speak of Babel, in perpetuity,
while I breast the waves, the Hellespont!

The Secret Poems of Fanny Brawne
(1800-1865)
(fiancée of John Keats)

1. The Sonnet
(December 1820)

Je t'aime, my Johnny. On my heart
Are these words deep-stamped like a French *cachet.*
Still faintly odored, like a French sachet
Refusing from its sweetness yet to part,
Remembering the poems I saw you start
From just some jest I made, your Morgan le Fay.
"Glory and loveliness have pass'd away,"
In youth you wrote, then aged it into art
That tapped medieval ores, romantic veins,
That built, in your small garden, fabled towers.
Friends of yours—no friends of mine—think us tragic.
"She is only Fashion's folly," they complain.
Your nightingale and thrush give my nights their hours;
I dream, like Madeline, of young love's magic.

11. A Memoriam for John Keats

(Written 1851-52, thirty years after his death in 1821)

"And thank God it has come!"
Those were the final words he spoke.
So Joseph wrote us, and evoked
John's ready spirit as he died.

No easy Grace for this proud soul
Who knew the scalpel, science's pen,
Who read the veins, the lines of men,
Then breathed fine odes, his life work's goal.

No easy Faith for one who knew
Early deaths of father, mother,
Who nursed his young, dying brother,
Then fought, though fevered, to outdo

The signs of mortality's sting:
His own coughed blood, his hectic face,
Fatigue that slowed his traveler's pace,
The pain that circled with its ring

Tighter than our affianced state.
A rare carnelian, bone white,
To cool his fever in the night,
I gave to John, to demonstrate

Our love, though hard, would long endure.
And so it has. Six years I mourned.
My friends grew tired to see me sworn
To Death as bride, and for a cure

Took me to plays for scenes of mirth.
And Edouart cut my silhouette.
I confess . . . I began to abet
Them. Yes, I stepped toward my rebirth.

Twice times six years I was alone
Before a husband, children came.
Not John's voice, not his face or name—
But they are now my art, my own.

Disciples come, as thick as leaves,
Declaring John beyond compare.
I think them right, though late. I wear
My paisley dress with lace-bound sleeves.

The scholars come to seek me out.
Now twenty winters—more—have passed.

They ask his life, they raise a glass
To John, whom critics flayed about
His youthful verses—crude, inept—
Though treasured now, like child's first steps
Towards mastery of artful leaps,
Unrecognized when he just crept.

Deserved, new his fame. Desired, his rest.
He wrote (one of his fond, last good-byes):
"I shall follow you with my eyes
Over the Heath." Loving bequest. And I am blest.

III. The Letter
(1864, one year before her death)

We burned my letters—hot, quick fire shriveling
All the flame-penned words spilled over the sheets.
No, only my words—they were none of his—
Of compromising boldness, words in lust,
Not lady-like, refined, no poet's lines
Semi-shawled in densely figured verse.
"For your future, your defense." That's what he said.
Oh God, the heat! He stooped, trembling, flushed,
Insistent, building up the cold night's fire
That made me crave the more to mold him close . . .
Yes, Frances Mary, your brother, our sweet John,
Who knew the colors of blood, of his, and of mine
On spotted linens that I soaked in chill brine . . .

You and I are too old to blush or burn,
Too old to remember the words of letters meant . . .
Except for one I hid, and later sent
To Rome, where it lay, unopened, read
Only by worms working his cool, cool tomb.

"The Secret Poems of Fanny Brawne" ByLine *Top Ten Award 2003*

MOTHERS AND SONS

In Case of Bears Canzone

Yellowstone Park—I can hardly bear
to contemplate each wild thing there: open range
for *carpe diem* buffaloes that bear
their heavy shawls like stocky Sherpa bear-
ers, that graze like glaciers in the moment
extended. But buffaloes can never be bears.
That statement can stand repeating, bear-
ing, as it does, on my state of mind,
or actually, being of many minds.
So, here goes: Buffaloes can never be bears.
Self evident, you claim. Not so. The wonder
is that not many people care to wonder

how categories tend to blunt the wonder
quotient of the animal, mammal named "bear."
Consider: Annie Sullivan was a wonder,
but she couldn't deflect bullets like Wonder
Woman. You think that's not a big enough range?
Do you remember the Seven Wonders
of the World? No pyramid is the wonder-
ous Great Wall of China. Think for a moment.
Science says the Big Bang was a moment
in time. Can our friend, Alice in Wonder-
land, snacking on mushrooms, get her mind
around the notion that it's all in her mind?

But there are other stories that are mind-
blowing. "Thaumaturgus" means a wonder-
worker, like Bishop Gregory, whose mind
moved a mountain. Was it because his mind-
set was on God, and saints must learn to bear
deflected praise, that he didn't lose his mind
but found a miracle? Let's call it mind
over matter, Greg as Power Ranger,
metaphysically using God's great range
finder to focus love. In my mind's
eye I see a matador at his moment of truth:
Will he make the kill? Moment-

ous only to those caught up in the moment,
carried away by the crowd's collective mind.
Where were you when Kennedy died? A moment
of silence, please. Imagine the moment
the sun first rose over Stonehenge. Wonder-
struck Druids making the most of the moment.
A moment is a moment is a moment?
So here we are, back to buffaloes and bears.
Aristotle knew how to think about bears:
As each one changes from moment to moment,
As each one grows and explores its ranges,
There is a constant we could call a range

light, like a guide for ships that are rang-
ing off course. This means, at any moment,
a channel to follow within the seas' ranges,
a "bearness" to follow, within forest ranges.
"Matter remains; form changes its mind."
Thus, when we discuss Himalayan ranges,
or Green Berets (who are not Texas Rangers),
or that pumpernickel cannot be Wonder
Bread, don't be surprised, don't even wonder
if I start to tear up, or hum "Home on the Range"
because I remember a small nighttime bear
my son called Teddy. Little lost-time bear.

It is this quiddity we strive to bear
by climbing Pike's Peak, not a whole mountain range,
which becomes a decision of moment,
an act of will, as we meet our own minds.
Buffaloes can never be bears? I wonder.

Sky Blue Waters Award 2003
Published in Möbius *2004 and*
In Case of Bears *by Peggy C. Hall 2006*

Sonnet One

I am a bear. Hath not a bear a nose?
Hath not a teddy eyes, two ears, two arms?
And though my fur is green, do you suppose
All creatures sport the hue of deep earthworm?
If those around you point to my stuffed chest
As evidence that I may lack a heart,
If they see my stitched mouth, my mid-seamed breast
As mindless bits of fabric or just as art,
Will you defend me? Say what we both know?
The gift I give is spaceless timeless love—
The love that runs through all, above, below,
Through rocks and trees that stand, comets that move.
I quote the Bard, whose words are worthy gold:
"To me, fair friend, you never can be old."

Published in The Greenbear Chronicles *by Sandra Riley 2000, 2005 and* In Case of Bears *by Peggy C. Hall 2006*

To the Daughter I Never Had

We are such whores, we mothers to our sons.
                              Everyone
has wept Jocasta's lines, in thought if not
                    in deed, subplot
being our tyrant sex that wombs and cups
the boy, expels the girl, and gives her up

to reenact such nonsense.   Mother, know
                    that your *tableau*
of *Pieta* I forgive.   So please tell
                    (you do it so well)
how Brother was your lovingest child
with caresses, cheek pats, deep-dimpled smile.

Is it his arms you want as I put you to bed?
                    And when you're fed
such lovely groceries I paid for in years
                    you are in tears
at a mem'ry of one Mother's Day meal:
A *bon voyage* supper, where he said, "We'll

keep in touch, Mom."? His wives wrote the cards
                    mailed from Asgard

▶

that I place in the bowl that he bought you, at nine,
                                        chipped, but still fine,
and patiently await (not to be outdone)
a card from my only begotten son.

ByLine *First Place 2003*
Sky Blue Waters Award 2003

Sometimes, There's a Gift

I saw it, lyin' there off to the side,
but passed it by, as no truck of me or mine.
See, I had more important fish to fry
at a place I didn't want to see or be—
Harlan County Hospital—back in the hills,
deep in those steep hollows of Kentucky.
Sure, the new road was straighter. Yeah, less scenic.
But safer? Ha. I was drivin' faster than I
had over the rutted back ways to McRoberts,
slippin' off at 17 to see my new girl—
"My girl," 's what I called my mom, at least
I did for a very long time. She told
'bout my little boy hands pattin' her cheeks,
'bout how I was her "lovin'est child."
Story for the kinfolks, at every cemetery "meet."
My sisters must have heard it ten too many times.

I stopped to pick up that cat on the way back,
though it looked like a half-plucked, wet chicken,
and she took right away to my mom's house,
though my mom had never allowed animals inside.
My mom couldn't speak. She seemed so asleep,
unable to offer a piece of her mind.
But it felt fit to call the cat "Boots,"
(a nickname my grandpa tacked on my mom,

▶

when he wasn't callin' her "Bunk" for Bernice).
Boots kept me company in the quiet house
as she grew out silk-long fur, raised dark paws
to be lifted each time I came in the door,
each night the six weeks before my mom died.

Doubling Back

Some nights I wake up misaligned. Resigned
by dawn, I roundabout like an old dog
trying to find "the spot," that X in my mind
that shines, a sun-struck tent. I dialogue
with the teabag packs. Drinking Earl Gray "bog"
is an old habit from college books, refined
on tours abroad, in City-centre travelogues.
Some nights I wake up misaligned, resigned
to creaking gears. E mail from my ex. By nine
I know I've won Cracker Jacks' tops, prologue
to amazing plots that will seem asinine
by night. I roundabout, like an old dog
with no traffic to cross. Then noon brings backlog.
Meet at the gym? Pick-Up Sticks? Too much combined.
Smocked words or plain? Right turn here? On I slog,
trying to find "the spot," that X in my mind
so mystifying that I once consigned
it to hormones. My role as a pedagogue
de-dunced that myth, like a stalagmite
that shines, a sun-struck tent. I monologue
at dusk to a round-stoned moon, analogue
to stocks whose pie charts wax and wane. I find
a bracelet from my mid-life son. A frog
charm. Plus a pearl. He had it designed . . . .
Some nights I wake up realigned.

Oregon State Poetry Annual Contest First Place
Published in Verseweavers *2003*

COME TO YOUR SENSES

Watch Out
for the
Little Green Men

*"At the fantastically decorated and enigmatic Rosslyn
Chapel in Midlothian [Scotland], there are 103 Green
Men in all."*
Jimmy Harte, *The Green Man*

Why do they make us feel scrutinized?
Their eyes follow us down brooding stone naves
of cathedrals, or peer from parish walls,
or guard figured sideboards in medieval halls.
Some, noseless, stare from ancient, moss-dank graves.
What are the fears we fear to verbalize?

For only their faces are realized,
as if the craftsmen wanted to save
pure artistry for Nature's forms, like cauls
of hawthorne, oak, or twining plants that crawl
and sprout from cheeks dark-bearded or close-shaved.
What does each foliaged head symbolize?

➤

➤

Truly the Green Men often seem agonized
by strangling vines that clasp to enslave
crude human flesh: eyes, ears, nose, and mouth all
changing to autumn's hues, falling
brown into fields still tipped with golden waves.
Are Green Men reminders that we fertilize

the fecund earth, whether uncouth or "civilized"?
But what about one Green Man who looks like a suave
young noble, in dapper cap to enthrall
eager May maidens, before Spring's nightfall?
Sins of the flesh, a perfidious knave?
Or is he Life-love idealized?

And what do the oldest Men memorialize?
They glare from high roof bosses, from architraves,
with pagan bared grins, lidless eyes appalled,
self-aware of feral menace. Our footfalls
intrude on their interleaved spaces. They've
scared us to leave, though we stand mesmerized

by what sculptors of Green Men emblemized,
by what carvers captured, designed, engraved:
We all die, whether in slum or Whitehall,
but, live, transformed, by Spring's siren call.
We should face our own faces in church or in caves.
Truth hides in Truth, cleverly leaf-disguised.

Quinella

If you can't hear it, see it,

and if you can't see it, be it,

just use your nose to smell
it well,

      for touching even
one taste of Eden
can never be a waste,
even, sometimes,
quintessence.

A Visit to My Oculist (for Prednisolone, Acetone, Opthalmic Suspension 1%)

We see eye to eye on the future:
Clear up the clouded crystal balls.
Everywhere one looks, there are eyesores
overseen by Dr. T. J. Eckleburg
whose *enormous*
yellow
spectacles
view only the *Valley of Ashes*.

Prednisolone

As I lay eyes on the frying pan
of his monocle
the doc says, "Keep an eye on my earlobe."
Then deerlights stun.

Saturn's swirling hula-hoops,
Comets' whipping tails,
Jackson Pollock's spatters,
Neon hubcap trails.

►

Acetone

"Quite an eyeful, the universe,"
the disembodied doctor quips,
"and now for a real eye opener!"
> Dew drops to dilate
> Peeping through the crystalline lens
> Behind the green iris
> Deltas of red rills
> Pasted on white globes.

This is Cap'n Nemo speaking
from under a bleary fathom or two
My sub's at your command,
Look at your watery view!

> "Take two drops on the hour,
> get a driver, wear dark glasses.
> We'll keep an eye on you."

I'm waiting for the scrim to rise

Ophthalmic Suspension 1%

Rock of Ages

*"An early jazz pianist who worked with singer Billie Holiday
said: 'Billie would sometimes come at a note from a long way off.'"*

Betty Edwards
Drawing on the Artist Within

I am discomposed today
    reading chaos theory
which explains randomness as order, for God's sake,
upsetting all my apple-cart notions
of up and down,
the ill-, the dis-, and the un-
becoming legitimate, legible, organized, usual, and true.
Question: Am I the only unstable force
                    left in the universe?

I am fit to be tied today
    those "super strings" holding the cosmos together
seem loopy to me,
certainly unapproved by UPS,
which always stamps RIGHT SIDE UP
unless they post it
to the space station.
Question: Why is the word "upright" defined
                as "up AND down"?

➤

➤

I am a law-abiding citizen
    but how can I observe the Laws
when quantum mechanics break them
and then quote Wordsworth's mantra:
" . . . of all the mighty world
of eye and ear, both what they half-create,
and what perceive"?
Question: When a tree falls in the forest, am I
                                    thinking about lunch?

But mostly I am disconcerted
    after learning from the physicists
that planets in orbit do
"Sing" their speeds, herald their notes.
So, attuning to the Harmony of the Spheres
is less a myth than it is
a matter of hearing aids.

Question:

    So,

    what **was** the opening number of God's Big Band?

New River Poets Award 2003
Poets at Work Award 2005

NATURE'S NATURE

The Ides of August

Everybody knows about July's "dog days":
Hot, every-butt-jump-in-the-pool days,
or lie supine in the shade, surrounded
by beach books bought, unread, doomed to be trashed,
or sit-on-the-tarmac-for-four-hour delays,
waitin' to fly away to cooler climes
as the Dog-Star, Sirius, rules the sky.

And August? I propose the title "cat days":
With a lot of surprises, a bit schizoid,
August deserves its own revered totem.
First, you don't see cats jumpin' into the pool!
No, they're about the sudden joy of gifts.
That bloated dead bird on your welcome mat,
like the proposed tax bill, elicits "Oh, Wow!"

Next, we all know whom a cat loves: the feeder.
So, we shouldn't be so startled when
kids in school uniforms rap on the glass
to beg our funds for their team's wish list,
and as far as mail solicitations,
my informal, one-person poll shows
that August is the hungriest month.

►

For even though you're still lyin' around
taking a cat-nap when and where you can,
they know the fall season, schedules, and school
all have to be planned. Torn between seasons,
you pounce on sales ads. Before it rains cats and dogs,
you run down the list for your hurricane stash
as you eye Labor Day as the last play date.

Stretching and yawning, you think, "Hold your kittens!"
And pop in that summer movie you'll sleep through.
Awakened by the UPS man, you'll push
your litter to one side, ignoring hints
from the dirty dishes that somebody needs to
beware the ides of August, those awful cat days.

Chant

Hold on to your hats,
Hurricane's a comin'.
Hurricane's a comin'.
Hurricane's a comin'.

Satellites spread the news:
Africa is sending westward,
Toward the islands, Allah's breath,
Ogun's whisper, Yewah's sigh.
Hold on to your Sunday hats,
Hurricane's a comin'.

Ships and autos on the move:
Lord, help harbors hold them all.
A million car-ants scurry inward
Toward the mainland's teeming heart.
Hold on to your steering wheel,
Hurricane's a comin'.

Waters sweep the sea lanes clear.
Trees and tides lift up their arms.
Wild creatures rush to hide
In hunkered places, like the people.
Hold on close to love handles,
Hurricane's a comin'.

Hold on to the generators,
Hold on to the brooms and tarps,
Hold on to the bathroom door,
Hold on to your little ones,
Hold on to your tears,
Hurricane is here.

ByLine *Award 2003*

Ever After, in the Everglades

Wild River of Grass, may you ever be
wild! River of Grass,
                    guard your secret heart
with distance and fear. The long drive, predawn start
made me feel like a paratrooper, stuffed
into a paneled truck, perched on scuffed
manatee-weight coolers, with crowded campers
chanting Sierra Club mantras, lungs amped:

> "Nature lovers lightly trek,
> not looking back, not back."

Wild River of Grass, may you ever be
wild! River of Grass,
                    teach us neophytes.
Like Everglades' airplants (called aerophytes),
I depended on rain, dust, and air,
the B.S. of new friends eager to share.
They said
        "Easy trip. We'll take care of you."
But the swamp intervened, all impromptu.
Nature sometimes bushwhacks,

        Not looking back, not back.

➤

89

Wild River of Grass, may you ever be
wild! River of Grass,
                    urge go-go guides
to stay closer to new paddlers, inside
tippy canoes that tangle with mangroves,
whose branches create tunnels of mauve,
murky light. In the gloom, I was in trouble.
The path I followed? Just vanishing bubbles.
Nature flows over tracks,

Not looking back, not back.

Wild River of Grass, may you ever be
wild! River of Grass,
                    dole out your surprises,
like fierce bugs, or canoes that capsize
into waist-high muck, like sawgrass that cuts
hands, face, and shins, or small sharks that butt
your boat in a bay. We beached on Cape Sable.
Friends laughed, helped pitch my tent; I wasn't able.
Nature evokes wisecracks,

Not looking back, not back.

Wild River of Grass, may you ever be
wild! River of Grass,
                 my compliments
to you! Even though red ants slept in my tent,
and, in the night, high tide became my guest …

Friends ask me,

      "What do you remember best?"

Pale grassy water, dawn birds on wet sand,
that infinite moment I felt graced and
Nature filled my rucksack,
Not looking back, not back.

LIVING AND DYING

Zap

Little piss ants, biting me while I write,
I pity you, but not so much. I squash
      Your tiny bodies
Into nothingness, *nada* on my plastic table
Bringing, for the instant, some revenge from
      Knowing
My life, of necessity, must sometimes
      Piss off
      Somebody.

When Your Number's Up

Others may buy Jimmy Choo. I buy sheets.
Usually in sets, but sometimes not,
but never white, oh please not white,
for Clorox leeches them beyond the pale,
though they do press up smart to pillow-slip your hair.
I don't care.

I choose Mexican colors, or Bangalese,
rusty rich, pumpkin-red, terra cotta clays,
or old, old, really old golds, paisley-splashed
patterns to spiral beyond the first sleep.
But I'm careful sheets don't cover my toes,
for toes know

the difference between life and deep death.
Yes, I choose a plus-300-thread count
for the "little death's" time, night's fleshy leap
toward fire-alive softness, dream-dancing feet . . .

I won't need any fancy shoes.
Just use my best sheets
for Death's last conceit.

Nude Ascending a Staircase
(Au Naturelle at 95)

She rides, she rides before my eyes, horse high—
Stepping the cobbles, no mobs to see her lovely hair
Draped there, half hiding breasts and nude thighs . . .
Take that quilt away! Let my feet protrude
From the sheets. My great-granddaughter brought the treats.
Chocolate creams, in the drawer. The mall seems
The preferred crowd for kids, interlude
Between school and bed. No multitudes for me . . .
Five, in low rapidity, chant and drum.
Sweat lodge humidity streaks bare chests
No rest, for we run to plunge into the trough
Spirit sisters, not lewd, but never subdued
By professions or others' views of sanctitude . . .
No, no—cooler water, please! A sponge bath is fine.
Forgive my lapses in lucidity.
I will go in nudity—to my death, I mean,
So the hospital gown is quite enough
And more than we wore *when it rained that day*
And topless we picked in thimbleberry bushes
Wild Western mountain meadowy fruits . . .
You'll bring my Jell-O soon? Oh. Pea soup. Lime-green *as Spring*
A season I sat, or rather, I posed
As you colored, in paints, flesh-tone tints

➤

My arms, natural hips and stark-naked eyes
Exposed to your maleness, creative lies
Rescuing me from gratuitous prudery . . .
Intruding on my nap? Never, my dear.
The priest is here, you say? Or should you play
Madonna's "Evita"? Am I in the mood
For songs or platitudes? Does prayer
Preclude a state of nature? *Or deny*
Gypsy Rose Lee, even the Goddess, who'd
Skinny-dip on Abaco's coral-hued beach
As we did, in my reaches through the past,
Dreaming mother-naked skin oh raw tasty food...

Alabama Writers' Conclave First Place Award 2004
New River Poets Award 2004
Published in Alalitcom *2004 and in* Watermarks *2007*

In Coming Years

May I be much more sensible,
exhaust every comprehensible
cell, dispense with deterrent keys,
carry my five senses in a thin valise,
and extract my body's rapt tangibles

until death, that ostensible
lack of receptors apprehensible.

Abstractions rely too much on heart's-ease.

    May I be much more

aware, with eyes and ears extensible
to nose and throat and hand, expandable
toward that fabled sixth sense.
                  O please
may I know soul synaesthesia,
be more than the sum of my portable partibles.

    May I be much more?

NOT ALWAYS WHAT IT SEEMS

On the Fence
Or
What's the View from Space?

It seems unfriendly if you build a fence.

A hedgerow, though porous, is still a wall,
and barricades the police erect incense
protestors who have come to yip and yawl,
to link their arms together, to convince
the public that statesmen orate to stall
the levee projects that, in good conscience,
should have been higher, lest flooding befall
a city buttressed mainly by pretense.

But weather (and cats) have the wherewithal
to overcome barriers. Their presence
shows us that circumvallations, as tall
as China's, Hadrian's, Israel's defense,
or just some backyard wooden slats, a small
token of close separations, sequenced
across the globe, wherever suburbs sprawl
and neighbors guard belongings, their romances—
from space, their awful grandeur seems to pall.

All palisades, eventually, must fall.
The Berlin Wall came down, but not by chance,
and so must checkpoints in Iraq. The call
to arms should be replaced by commonsense
rethinking of the purposes for walls,
and good reasons for their deterrence:

To keep children safe, overall,
protect performers from their audiences,
encircle animals that prey or maul.

So, let's build more gates, with less forbiddance,
instead of detaining the world behind Fear's wall.

* *The Great Wall is the only man-made structure seen with the naked eye from space.*

Up in Arms

Whether they're nursed, rehearsed, or cleavage-parted,
mammary glands play their role in debates,
and, more or less, have always been in our faces.
Yes, we keep abreast of the current, the newest,
like armored vests for soldiers who left
babies at home while they're nursing arms

in Iraq, trying to reduce that arm
of al Qaeda blowing bodies into parts,
like a breastless torso, no function left,
not even a head with which to debate
which divisive quarrel is old or new.
My God, what is it we should squarely face?

Look at art—say Venus de Milo's face.
And what about her fair, but broken arms?
Beautiful, yes! But they weren't what was new.
Hellenic Greeks welcomed the "high breasts" part,
so art critics say, as they fiercely debate
the date female nudity curved to the left.

Hey, did Greek sculptors become Left-wingers?
What had happened to Helen, with "the face
that launched a thousand ships"? Today, debaters
still do battle over breasts, Third-world arms-
races overshadowed, for the most part,
by Victoria Secret's newcomer

bra, so linger-in-the-lingerie news!
Let's make a clean breast of it: leftover
Puritans interpret "a man of parts"
as one with a good mind and clever face.
No hitting-below-the-belt jokes, just arm-
punching-arm sexism to milk the debate

called Janet's "Nipplegate." Oh, that debate—
or Madonna's, or Hilary's—no longer newsworthy?
Oh my, what is a post-feminist's coat-of-arms?
If burn-the-bra is *passé,* what is left
except to look a person full in the face
and let one's best bra buy do its part:

To uplift debates, whether Right or Left,
to give burkaed women new shapes, not faces,
to augment our logic—plus our other parts.

at face value

At Face Value

at face value

At Face Value

At Face Value

at face value

AT FACE VALUE

At Face Value

AT   FACE   VALUE

at face value

at face value

at face value

at face value – At Face Value

at face value - At Face Value

at face value - At Face Value

At Face Value

At Face Value

At Face Value

Dime-sized cheek spot:
"Mole Face" they taunted.
I was a shy child, wanting to
Be worth
More than a dime.

From Left to Right
Back Row: Jason Stoetzer, Travis Neff

Middle Row: Laverne Lewis-Cuzzocrea, Teresa Barceló, Tiffany 'Hanan' Madera,
T. L. Brown, Peggy C. Hall with Gus Greenbear, Ellen Haynes,
Soledad Centurión Yedro, Ray Sullivan, Sandra Riley.

Bottom Row: Jennifer Stewart, Rudi Goblen, Ana Mendez, Odell Rivas.

Odell Rivas photo by Bob Lasky

Peggy C. Hall has earned awards in contests sponsored by *ByLine Magazine, Writer's Digest,* the National League of Pen Women, the Alabama Writers' Conclave, the National Federation of State Poetry Societies and others. Her poems have appeared in publications such as *English Journal, Frost Notes, Bibliophilos, Möbius, Pikeville Review, The Anthology of New England Writers,* and *Sincerely Elvis.* She lives in Miami, Florida with Sandra Riley, sister-cats Popsy and Threebee, and a 27-gram parakeet named Alexander the Great.

www.ingramcontent.com/pod-product-compliance
Lightning Source LLC
Chambersburg PA
CBHW051833040426
42447CB00006B/511

* 9 7 8 0 9 6 6 6 5 3 1 0 9 1 *